AGE

OF

JUSTICE

Volume V

By
W.D. Palmer

AuthorHouse™
1663 Liberty Drive
Bloomington, IN 47403
www.authorhouse.com
Phone: 833-262-8899

This book is printed on acid-free paper.

ISBN: 978-1-6655-1404-0 (sc)
ISBN: 978-1-6655-1405-7 (e)

Print information available on the last page.

Published by AuthorHouse 01/20/2021

author HOUSE

Walter D. Palmer Leadership School

Currently W. D. Palmer is the founder and director of the W. D. Palmer Foundation (est. 1955), a repository of information-gathering on racism in health, education, employment, housing, courts, prisons, higher education, military, government, politics, law, banking, insurance, etc.

He is also the founder of the Black People's University of Philadelphia (1955) Freedom School, which was the grassroots organizing and training center for grassroots community and political leadership in Philadelphia and nationally. These organizations were run as nonprofit unincorporated associations from 1955 until 1980, when the Palmer Foundation received its 501(c)(3) federal tax exemption status.

W. D. Palmer has also been a professor, teaching American Racism at the University of Pennsylvania since the 1960's and today he is a member of the Presidents Commission on 1619, the 400-year anniversary of African slavery in America.

Professor Palmer has been a social activist leading the fight against racial injustice for over seventy years in Philadelphia and around the nation. In 2018, Philadelphia honored him for the organizing work he did to reform the Philadelphia school system in 1967.

In 2020, Philadelphia honored him for 65 years of fighting for social justice throughout the country. In 1980, he led the fight for parental school choice which helped the Governor of Pennsylvania get a law passed in 1997, and in 2000 he created the Walter D. Palmer Leadership Charter School.

In 2005, he borrowed eleven million dollars to build a 55 thousand square-foot two story building on two acres of land in North Philadelphia, which was donated to the school by the City of Philadelphia, and because of the school's rapid growth, in 2010 he acquired the Saint Bartholomew Catholic High School, for his middle and high school.

In ten years, the school grew from three hundred elementary and middle school students, to two hundred preschoolers and over a thousand kindergarten to twelfth graders. In 2005, W. D. Palmer commissioned a muralist to paint over four hundred pre-selected portraits on the school walls, corridors, and stairwells, with a goal to paint thirty fifteen foot murals in the gymnatorium.

Although the Walter D. Palmer Leadership School recruited "at risk children" that were from seventeen of the poorest zip codes in Philadelphia and 300 percent below poverty, the school boasted of a 95% daily attendance, 100% high school graduation, and 100% post graduate placement in four year and two year colleges, trade and technology schools, or military, until the school's closing in 2015.

Property Of

Name: _____

Address: _____

_____

Phone: _____

Email: _____

Emergency Contact: _____

_____

Acknowledgement

I would like to take this time to acknowledge from the beginning of the Palmer Foundation, 1955, the many contributors who helped to gather information, organize, and write the leadership, self-development, and social awareness curriculums.

From the Palmer Foundation's inception, these contributors have been composed of community members, elementary, middle- and high-school students, as well as college student volunteers and interns, along with professional contributors.

We chose this method and process because it was consistent with our history, vision, philosophy, mission, and goals of always developing leadership in practice.

These groups, who have helped to produce our materials, are the same cohorts who over the years have helped to teach and train others as well as helped to develop a national database through which these curriculum and training materials can be distributed.

The story of the Palmer Foundation is the story of building community and leadership at the same time, and the Palmer Foundation wants to give an enthusiastic endorsement in recognition of the thousands of people who have been with us on this long and arduous journey.

We want to take this time to thank the many community leaders and people that have invited us into their communities to help them reclaim and restore the many values, properties, and people who may have been threatened with the loss of finance, property, and life, because they are the true heroes and heroines that made the Palmer Foundation the success that it has become.

Public Appeal

The Palmer Foundation is a federal 501(c)(3) organization that has spent over 65 years educating and fighting for social justice in the most underserved "at risk" communities around the country. Our goals have always been to use education for human liberation and encourage "at risk" families and children to help gather, write, produce, publish, and teach others in a similar situation.

Our mission is to disseminate our leadership, self-development, social justice, and grassroots-organizing books, manuals, and learning materials across America and around the world.

Our goals are to sell these publications or to offer them in exchange for a suggested tax-exempt donation that would allow us to continue producing our leadership training, as well as grassroots community and political organizing efforts.

Ultimately, we would like to create a satellite school as a model or prototype of the Walter D. Palmer Leadership School that could be replicated around the world, and we appeal for your enthusiastic and sustained support going forward.

Table of Contents

INTRODUCTION

DR. PALMER, DISTINGUISHED PROFESSOR AND LIFELONG SOCIAL CHANGE ACTIVIST, ONE DAY ENCOUNTERS A MYSTERIOUS MAN WHO SAYS HIS NAME IS *MR. JAMES*...

AFTER BEFRIENDING DR. PALMER, MR. JAMES MYSTERIOUSLY DISAPPEARS. BUT BEFORE HE DOES, HE LEAVES DR. PALMER HIS FAVORITE WATCH.

AS DR. PALMER DISCOVERS, THE WATCH CONTAINS A HIDDEN *POWER DIAL*, WHICH ALLOWS HIM TO TRANSFORM FROM A 75-YEAR-OLD PROFESSOR INTO A REPLICA OF HIMSELF AT AGES 20, 30, 40, AND 50 – AT DIFFERENT STAGES OF HIS STRUGGLE FOR SOCIAL CHANGE.

I AM MR. JAMES. ALTHOUGH DR. PALMER DOES NOT KNOW IT YET, MYSELF AND OTHER EXTRA-CELESTIAL *AGENTS OF AGE* HAVE BEEN OBSERVING HIS LIFELONG STRUGGLE FOR SOCIAL CHANGE. WE WANT TO SUPPORT HIS EFFORTS.

DR. PALMER RECEIVES INSTRUCTIONS THAT HE MUST RETURN THE POWER DIAL IN NO MORE THAN 25 YEARS, WHEN HE REACHES AGE 100.

IN THE MEANTIME, HE HAS FULL USE OF THE POWER DIAL'S ABILITIES, AS WELL AS A RANGE OF OTHER DEVICES AND THE HELP OF SEVERAL SUPERNATURAL CREATURES, TO AID HIM IN HIS FIGHT FOR SOCIAL CHANGE.

TOPIC DEFINITION

EACH OF THE FOLLOWING PAGES IS FOCUSED ON A PARTICULAR SOCIETAL ISSUE.

EVERY TOPIC HAS A DEFINITION, INTENDED TO PROVIDE AN OVERVIEW AND BASIC FACTS AND STATISTICS.

THE GOAL OF THESE DEFINITIONS IS TO ENCOURAGE STUDENTS TO THINK ABOUT THE ISSUES AND TO PURSUE FURTHER RESEARCH AND LEARNING.

ULTIMATELY, WE WANT YOUNG PEOPLE TO THINK CREATIVELY AND FOR THEMSELVES ABOUT HOW TO RESPOND TO THESE ISSUES.

WHERE TO TURN?

EACH OF THE FOLLOWING PAGES CONTAINS A FORM WITH THE TITLE "WHERE TO TURN?" AND BLANK SPACES FOR CONTACT INFORMATION AT CITY, STATE, COUNTY, AND NATIONAL LEVELS.

STUDENTS ARE ENCOURAGED TO RESEARCH AND FILL OUT THESE FORMS, WITH THE HELP OF THEIR PARENTS AND TEACHERS. IN THIS WAY, STUDENTS, PARENTS, AND TEACHERS WILL EDUCATE THEMSELVES AND EACH OTHER WHILE GETTING INVOLVED IN THE PROJECT.

AFTER FILLING OUT THE "WHERE TO TURN" INFORMATION ON EACH PAGE, STUDENTS WILL HAVE PERSONALIZED BOOKLETS WITH THEIR OWN THINKING AND RESEARCH INSIDE.

SCHOOL DROPOUT

 DR. PALMER, DISTINGUISHED PROFESSOR AND LIFELONG SOCIAL CHANGE ACTIVIST, ENCOUNTERS A MYSTERIOUS MAN CALLED MR. JAMES. UNKNOWN TO DR. PALMER, MR. JAMES IS AN *AGENT OF AGE*. PRIOR TO HIS DISAPPEARANCE, MR. JAMES LEAVES DR. PALMER HIS WRISTWATCH.

 THE WATCH, DR. PALMER DISCOVERS, CONTAINS A HIDDEN *POWER DIAL*, WHICH WILL ALLOW HIM TO TRANSFORM FROM A 75-YEAR-OLD PROFESSOR INTO A REPLICA OF HIMSELF AT AGES 20, 30, 40, AND 50. THE WATCH, ALONG WITH A RANGE OF OTHER DEVICES AND THE HELP OF SEVERAL SUPERNATURAL CREATURES, ARE MEANT TO AID HIM IN HIS FIGHT FOR SOCIAL CHANGE.

 AT AGE 20, DR. PALMER WAS AN *URBAN SURVIVALIST*, AN EXPERT AT NAVIGATING IN A TOUGH ENVIRONMENT AND LOOKING OUT FOR THOSE AROUND HIM.

NOW, HE USES THE POWER DIAL TO TRANFORM INTO HIS 20-YEAR-OLD SELF TO CONTINUE FIGHTING THE CHALLENGES HE CONFRONTED THEN.

POWER DIALS ARE THE SOURCE OF AN AGENT OF AGE'S ABILITIES. THEY ACT AS LINKS TO THE *GREATNESS OF TIME*.

DR. PALMER'S POWER DIAL ENABLES HIM TO *TRAVEL THROUGH TIME*. IT ALSO TELLS TIME ANYWHERE IN THE WORLD AND PROVIDES STATS ON ANY LOCAL ENVIRONMENT.

WHERE TO TURN?

WHERE SHOULD A YOUNG PERSON FACED WITH THIS ISSUE TURN? RESEARCH AND FILL OUT THE CONTACT INFORMATION BELOW.

IN YOUR CITY...
NAME: _____
PHONE: _____
EMAIL: _____

IN YOUR STATE...
NAME: _____
PHONE: _____
EMAIL: _____

IN YOUR COUNTY...
NAME: _____
PHONE: _____
EMAIL: _____

NATION-WIDE...
NAME: _____
PHONE: _____
EMAIL: _____

SCHOOL DROPOUT

SCHOOL DROPOUT IS WHEN STUDENTS LEAVE SCHOOL BEFORE GRADUATING. STUDENTS DROP OUT OF SCHOOL FOR MANY REASONS - FOR EXAMPLE, BECAUSE THEY ARE NOT ENGAGED IN WHAT THEY'RE LEARNING, BECAUSE THEY DON'T SEE SCHOOL AS RELEVANT TO THEIR LIVES, OR BECAUSE THEY FEEL PRESSURE TO EARN MONEY OR CARETAKE FOR A CHILD OR YOUNGER SIBLING.

SCHOOL DROPOUT RATES ARE VERY HIGH IN THE U.S. - ABOUT 25% OF FIRST-YEAR HIGH SCHOOL STUDENTS FAIL TO GRADUATE ON TIME.[1] IN ADDITION, THIS DROPOUT RATE VARIES BY RACE: BLACK AND HISPANIC STUDENTS ARE LESS LIKELY TO GRADUATE HIGH SCHOOL THAN ASIAN AND WHITE STUDENTS ARE.[2]

SEX TRAFFICKING

DR. PALMER, DISTINGUISHED PROFESSOR AND LIFELONG SOCIAL CHANGE ACTIVIST, ENCOUNTERS A MYSTERIOUS MAN CALLED MR. JAMES. UNKNOWN TO DR. PALMER, MR. JAMES IS AN **AGENT OF AGE**. PRIOR TO HIS DISAPPEARANCE, MR. JAMES LEAVES DR. PALMER HIS WRISTWATCH.

THE WATCH, DR. PALMER DISCOVERS, CONTAINS A HIDDEN **POWER DIAL**, WHICH WILL ALLOW HIM TO TRANSFORM FROM A 75-YEAR-OLD PROFESSOR INTO A REPLICA OF HIMSELF AT AGES 20, 30, 40, AND 50. THE WATCH, ALONG WITH A RANGE OF OTHER DEVICES AND THE HELP OF SEVERAL SUPERNATURAL CREATURES, ARE MEANT TO AID HIM IN HIS FIGHT FOR SOCIAL CHANGE.

AT AGE 30, DR. PALMER WAS A **BLACK POWER ACTIVIST**, WORKING LOCALLY AND NATIONALLY TO DEMAND JUSTICE.

NOW, HE USES THE POWER DIAL TO TRANFORM INTO HIS 30-YEAR-OLD SELF SO THAT HE CAN CONTINUE FIGHTING RACISM, DISCRIMINATION, AND HATE CRIMES.

ONE OF DR. PALMER'S DEVICES IS A PAIR OF **POWER SUNGLASSES**, WHICH PROVIDE HIM WITH DISTANT DAY AND NIGHT VISION AND ALLOW HIM TO SEE THROUGH DARKNESS, WALLS, RAIN, SNOW, AND DUST STORMS!

WHERE TO TURN?

WHERE SHOULD A YOUNG PERSON FACED WITH THIS ISSUE TURN? RESEARCH AND FILL OUT THE CONTACT INFORMATION BELOW.

IN YOUR CITY...

NAME: _____

PHONE: _____

EMAIL: _____

IN YOUR STATE...

NAME: _____

PHONE: _____

EMAIL: _____

IN YOUR COUNTY...

NAME: _____

PHONE: _____

EMAIL: _____

NATION-WIDE...

NAME: _____

PHONE: _____

EMAIL: _____

SEX TRAFFICKING

SEX TRAFFICKING IS HUMAN TRAFFICKING, OR MODERN-DAY SLAVERY, FOR THE PURPOSE OF SEXUAL EXPLOITATION.

HUMAN TRAFFICKING EARNS GLOBAL PROFITS OF ROUGHLY $150 BILLION A YEAR, $99 BILLION OF WHICH COMES FROM COMMERCIAL SEXUAL EXPLOITATION.[3]

IN 2018, OVER HALF OF THE HUMAN TRAFFICKING CASES ACTIVE IN THE U.S. WERE SEX TRAFFICKING CASES INVOLVING ONLY CHILDREN.[4] IN FACT, THE AVERAGE AGE A TEEN ENTERS THE SEX TRADE IS 12 TO 14 YEARS OLD. IN ADDITION, MANY OF THESE ARE RUNAWAY GIRLS WHO WERE SEXUALLY ABUSED AS CHILDREN.[5]

SEXUAL ASSAULT

DR. PALMER, DISTINGUISHED PROFESSOR AND LIFELONG SOCIAL CHANGE ACTIVIST, ENCOUNTERS A MYSTERIOUS MAN CALLED MR. JAMES. UNKNOWN TO DR. PALMER, MR. JAMES IS AN *AGENT OF AGE*. PRIOR TO HIS DISAPPEARANCE, MR. JAMES LEAVES DR. PALMER HIS WRISTWATCH.

THE WATCH, DR. PALMER DISCOVERS, CONTAINS A HIDDEN *POWER DIAL*, WHICH WILL ALLOW HIM TO TRANSFORM FROM A 75-YEAR-OLD PROFESSOR INTO A REPLICA OF HIMSELF AT AGES 20, 30, 40, AND 50. THE WATCH, ALONG WITH A RANGE OF OTHER DEVICES AND THE HELP OF SEVERAL SUPERNATURAL CREATURES, ARE MEANT TO AID HIM IN HIS FIGHT FOR SOCIAL CHANGE.

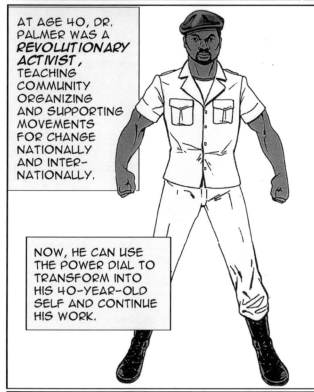

AT AGE 40, DR. PALMER WAS A *REVOLUTIONARY ACTIVIST*, TEACHING COMMUNITY ORGANIZING AND SUPPORTING MOVEMENTS FOR CHANGE NATIONALLY AND INTER-NATIONALLY.

NOW, HE CAN USE THE POWER DIAL TO TRANSFORM INTO HIS 40-YEAR-OLD SELF AND CONTINUE HIS WORK.

ONE OF DR. PALMER'S DEVICES IS A *POWER HEARING DEVICE*, WHICH CAN HEAR UP TO A MILE AWAY AND TRANSLATE ANY SPOKEN LANGUAGE INTO ENGLISH!

WHERE TO TURN?

WHERE SHOULD A YOUNG PERSON FACED WITH THIS ISSUE TURN? RESEARCH AND FILL OUT THE CONTACT INFORMATION BELOW.

IN YOUR CITY...

NAME: _____

PHONE: _____

EMAIL: _____

IN YOUR STATE...

NAME: _____

PHONE: _____

EMAIL: _____

IN YOUR COUNTY...

NAME: _____

PHONE: _____

EMAIL: _____

NATION-WIDE...

NAME: _____

PHONE: _____

EMAIL: _____

SEXUAL ASSAULT

SEXUAL ASSAULT IS ANY NONCONSENSUAL SEXUAL ACT, INCLUDING WHEN SOMEONE DOES NOT HAVE THE ABILITY TO CONSENT.

SEXUAL ASSAULT IS ESPECIALLY COMMON ON COLLEGE CAMPUSES. IN FACT, NEARLY 1 IN 4 FEMALE COLLEGE STUDENTS EXPERIENCE SEXUAL ASSAULT.[6] IN ADDITION, IT IS ESTIMATED THAT ONLY A SMALL PERCENTAGE OF SEXUAL ASSAULTS ON COLLEGE CAMPUSES ARE REPORTED.[7]

THE CONSEQUENCES OF SEXUAL ASSAULT ARE FAR-REACHING. FOR INSTANCE, 4 OUT OF 5 RAPE VICTIMS SUFFER FROM CHRONIC PHYSICAL OR PSYCHOLOGICAL CONDITIONS.[8] IN ADDITION, RAPE SURVIVORS ARE MORE LIKELY TO ATTEMPT SUICIDE THAN ARE NON-SURVIVORS.[9]

SEXUAL HARASSMENT

DR. PALMER, DISTINGUISHED PROFESSOR AND LIFELONG SOCIAL CHANGE ACTIVIST, ENCOUNTERS A MYSTERIOUS MAN CALLED MR. JAMES. UNKNOWN TO DR. PALMER, MR. JAMES IS AN **AGENT OF AGE.** PRIOR TO HIS DISAPPEARANCE, MR. JAMES LEAVES DR. PALMER HIS WRISTWATCH.

THE WATCH, DR. PALMER DISCOVERS, CONTAINS A HIDDEN **POWER DIAL,** WHICH WILL ALLOW HIM TO TRANSFORM FROM A 75-YEAR-OLD PROFESSOR INTO A REPLICA OF HIMSELF AT AGES 20, 30, 40, AND 50. THE WATCH, ALONG WITH A RANGE OF OTHER DEVICES AND THE HELP OF SEVERAL SUPERNATURAL CREATURES, ARE MEANT TO AID HIM IN HIS FIGHT FOR SOCIAL CHANGE.

AT AGE 50, DR. PALMER WAS AN **ACADEMIC ACTIVIST,** ADVOCATING ON BEHALF OF STUDENTS AND TEACHING REAL-WORLD LEADERSHIP SKILLS.

NOW, HE CAN USE THE POWER DIAL TO TRANFORM INTO HIS 50-YEAR-OLD SELF AND CONTINUE THIS WORK.

AMONG DR. PALMER'S DEVICES IS A **POWER BICYCLE,** WHICH HAS 12 SPEEDS AND CAN CLIMB HILLS AND MOUNTAINS!

WHERE TO TURN?

WHERE SHOULD A YOUNG PERSON FACED WITH THIS ISSUE TURN? RESEARCH AND FILL OUT THE CONTACT INFORMATION BELOW.

IN YOUR CITY...

NAME: _____

PHONE: _____

EMAIL: _____

IN YOUR STATE...

NAME: _____

PHONE: _____

EMAIL: _____

IN YOUR COUNTY...

NAME: _____

PHONE: _____

EMAIL: _____

NATION-WIDE...

NAME: _____

PHONE: _____

EMAIL: _____

SEXUAL HARASSMENT

SEXUAL HARASSMENT INCLUDES COMMENTS, GESTURES, OR ACTIONS THAT ARE FOCUSED ON A PERSON'S APPEARANCE OR BODY PARTS AND ARE INTENDED TO HURT OR INTIMIDATE. SEXUAL HARASSMENT MAY BE VERBAL OR PHYSICAL, OR IT MIGHT TAKE THE FORM OF UNWANTED CALLS OR TEXTS.

SEXUAL HARASSMENT IS ESPECIALLY COMMON IN THE WORKPLACE. ONE REPORT FOUND THAT OVER HALF OF WORKING WOMEN HAD EXPERIENCED SOME FORM OF SEXUAL HARASSMENT AT THEIR JOBS.[10] IN ADDITION, FOR THOSE WHO REPORTED HARASSMENT, THE MAJORITY FOUND THAT NOTHING CHANGED AFTER THEY REPORTED IT; SOME EVEN SAID THAT THE SITUATION WORSENED.[11]

SPECIAL EDUCATION

DR. PALMER, DISTINGUISHED PROFESSOR AND LIFELONG SOCIAL CHANGE ACTIVIST, ENCOUNTERS A MYSTERIOUS MAN CALLED MR. JAMES. UNKNOWN TO DR. PALMER, MR. JAMES IS AN **AGENT OF AGE**. PRIOR TO HIS DISAPPEARANCE, MR. JAMES LEAVES DR. PALMER HIS WRISTWATCH.

THE WATCH, DR. PALMER DISCOVERS, CONTAINS A HIDDEN **POWER DIAL**, WHICH WILL ALLOW HIM TO TRANSFORM FROM A 75-YEAR-OLD PROFESSOR INTO A REPLICA OF HIMSELF AT AGES 20, 30, 40, AND 50. THE WATCH, ALONG WITH A RANGE OF OTHER DEVICES AND THE HELP OF SEVERAL SUPERNATURAL CREATURES, ARE MEANT TO AID HIM IN HIS FIGHT FOR SOCIAL CHANGE.

ONE OF DR. PALMER'S SUPERNATURAL ALLIES IS A GERMAN SHEPHERD GUARD DOG NAMED **WOLF**.

WOLF'S COLLAR CONTAINS A POWER DIAL SIMILAR TO THE ONE IN DR. PALMER'S WATCH. THE POWER DIAL GIVES WOLF SUPERNATURAL ABILITIES INCLUDING **IMMORTAL LIFE!**

AMONG DR. PALMER'S DEVICES IS A **POWER SONAR DEVICE**, WHICH ALLOWS HIM TO DETECT OBJECTS UNDERWATER!

WHERE TO TURN?

WHERE SHOULD A YOUNG PERSON FACED WITH THIS ISSUE TURN? RESEARCH AND FILL OUT THE CONTACT INFORMATION BELOW.

IN YOUR CITY...

NAME: _____

PHONE: _____

EMAIL: _____

IN YOUR STATE...

NAME: _____

PHONE: _____

EMAIL: _____

IN YOUR COUNTY...

NAME: _____

PHONE: _____

EMAIL: _____

NATION-WIDE...

NAME: _____

PHONE: _____

EMAIL: _____

SPECIAL EDUCATION

SPECIAL EDUCATION SERVES STUDENTS WITH MENTAL, PHYSICAL, EMOTIONAL, AND BEHAVIORAL DISABILITIES.

IN THE U.S., NEARLY 14% OF ALL STUDENTS AGED 13-21 ARE SPECIAL EDUCATION STUDENTS.[19] THE MAJORITY OF THESE STUDENTS, HOWEVER, SPEND MOST OF THEIR TIME IN REGULAR EDUCATION CLASSES.

SOME OF THE MOST COMMON LEARNING DISABILITIES INCLUDE **DYSLEXIA** (A DISORDER THAT AFFECTS ABILITY TO READ), **ADHD** (A DISORDER THAT AFFECTS ABILITY TO CONCENTRATE), **DYSCALCULA** (A DISORDER THAT AFFECTS ABILITIES WITH MATH), AND **DYSGRAPHIA** (A DISORDER THAT AFFECTS ABILITY TO WRITE).

STDS

DR. PALMER, DISTINGUISHED PROFESSOR AND LIFELONG SOCIAL CHANGE ACTIVIST, ENCOUNTERS A MYSTERIOUS MAN CALLED MR. JAMES. UNKNOWN TO DR. PALMER, MR. JAMES IS AN *AGENT OF AGE*. PRIOR TO HIS DISAPPEARANCE, MR. JAMES LEAVES DR. PALMER HIS WRISTWATCH.

THE WATCH, DR. PALMER DISCOVERS, CONTAINS A HIDDEN *POWER DIAL*, WHICH WILL ALLOW HIM TO TRANSFORM FROM A 75-YEAR-OLD PROFESSOR INTO A REPLICA OF HIMSELF AT AGES 20, 30, 40, AND 50. THE WATCH, ALONG WITH A RANGE OF OTHER DEVICES AND THE HELP OF SEVERAL SUPERNATURAL CREATURES, ARE MEANT TO AID HIM IN HIS FIGHT FOR SOCIAL CHANGE.

AMONG DR. PALMER'S SUPERNATURAL ALLIES ARE THE *GUARDIAN GODS* OF ALL SEVEN CONTINENTS.

THE ARCTIC, *GUARDIAN OF WIND*, CAN REDIRECT WIND, STORMS, HURRICANES, AND CYCLONES TO ASSIST DR. PALMER!

ONE OF DR. PALMER'S DEVICES IS A *POWER SUBMARINE*, A HYPER-SUBMARINE THAT CAN REACH SPEEDS OF UP TO 50 MPH UNDERWATER!

WHERE TO TURN?

WHERE SHOULD A YOUNG PERSON FACED WITH THIS ISSUE TURN? RESEARCH AND FILL OUT THE CONTACT INFORMATION BELOW.

IN YOUR CITY...

NAME: _____

PHONE: _____

EMAIL: _____

IN YOUR STATE...

NAME: _____

PHONE: _____

EMAIL: _____

IN YOUR COUNTY...

NAME: _____

PHONE: _____

EMAIL: _____

NATION-WIDE...

NAME: _____

PHONE: _____

EMAIL: _____

STDS

SEXUALLY TRANSMITTED DISEASES, OR *STDS*, ARE INFECTIONS THAT SPREAD FROM PERSON TO PERSON DURING SEX.

STDS ARE CAUSED BY BACTERIA, PARASITES, AND VIRUSES. ANTIBIOTICS CAN TREAT STDS CAUSED BY BACTERIA OR PARASITES. THERE IS NO CURE FOR STDS CAUSED BY A VIRUS, BUT MEDICINES CAN OFTEN HELP WITH THE SYMPTOMS.

MANY STDS HAVE NO SYMPTOMS OR ONLY MILD SYMPTOMS IN SOME PEOPLE, SO A PERSON CAN HAVE AND SPREAD STDS WITHOUT KNOWING. HOWEVER, LEFT UNTREATED MOST STDS LEAD TO SERIOUS HEALTH CONDITIONS OR EVEN DEATH.

STEALING

DR. PALMER, DISTINGUISHED PROFESSOR AND LIFELONG SOCIAL CHANGE ACTIVIST, ENCOUNTERS A MYSTERIOUS MAN CALLED MR. JAMES. UNKNOWN TO DR. PALMER, MR. JAMES IS AN *AGENT OF AGE*. PRIOR TO HIS DISAPPEARANCE, MR. JAMES LEAVES DR. PALMER HIS WRISTWATCH.

THE WATCH, DR. PALMER DISCOVERS, CONTAINS A HIDDEN *POWER DIAL*, WHICH WILL ALLOW HIM TO TRANSFORM FROM A 75-YEAR-OLD PROFESSOR INTO A REPLICA OF HIMSELF AT AGES 20, 30, 40, AND 50. THE WATCH, ALONG WITH A RANGE OF OTHER DEVICES AND THE HELP OF SEVERAL SUPERNATURAL CREATURES, ARE MEANT TO AID HIM IN HIS FIGHT FOR SOCIAL CHANGE.

AMONG DR. PALMER'S SUPERNATURAL ALLIES ARE THE *GUARDIAN GODS* OF ALL SEVEN CONTINENTS.

AFRICA, THE *GUARDIAN OF THE EARTH,* FIGHTS FOR PROTECTION OF THE ENVIRONMENT AND CAN AID DR. PALMER BY PROVIDING SHELTERS AND BLOCKADES OF EARTH!

ONE OF DR. PALMER'S DEVICES IS A *POWER MOTORCYCLE,* WHICH CAN REACH SPEEDS OF UP TO 150 MPH!

WHERE TO TURN?

WHERE SHOULD A YOUNG PERSON FACED WITH THIS ISSUE TURN? RESEARCH AND FILL OUT THE CONTACT INFORMATION BELOW.

IN YOUR CITY...
NAME: _____
PHONE: _____
EMAIL: _____

IN YOUR STATE...
NAME: _____
PHONE: _____
EMAIL: _____

IN YOUR COUNTY...
NAME: _____
PHONE: _____
EMAIL: _____

NATION-WIDE...
NAME: _____
PHONE: _____
EMAIL: _____

STEALING

STEALING IS TAKING SOMETHING THAT BELONGS TO SOMEONE ELSE WITHOUT THEIR PERMISSION. COMMON FORMS OF STEALING INCLUDE:

SHOPLIFTING: TAKING SOMETHING FROM A STORE WITHOUT PAYING.

BURGLARY: STEALING SOMETHING FROM SOMEONE'S HOME.

PLAGIARISM: TAKING SOMEONE ELSE'S WORDS OR IDEAS WITHOUT PERMISSION OR WITHOUT GIVING THEM CREDIT.

IDENTITY THEFT: USING ANOTHER PERSON'S NAME, BANK ACCOUNT, OR CREDIT CARD INFORMATION WITHOUT PERMISSION.

SUICIDE

DR. PALMER, DISTINGUISHED PROFESSOR AND LIFELONG SOCIAL CHANGE ACTIVIST, ENCOUNTERS A MYSTERIOUS MAN CALLED MR. JAMES. UNKNOWN TO DR. PALMER, MR. JAMES IS AN **AGENT OF AGE**. PRIOR TO HIS DISAPPEARANCE, MR. JAMES LEAVES DR. PALMER HIS WRISTWATCH.

THE WATCH, DR. PALMER DISCOVERS, CONTAINS A HIDDEN **POWER DIAL**, WHICH WILL ALLOW HIM TO TRANSFORM FROM A 75-YEAR-OLD PROFESSOR INTO A REPLICA OF HIMSELF AT AGES 20, 30, 40, AND 50. THE WATCH, ALONG WITH A RANGE OF OTHER DEVICES AND THE HELP OF SEVERAL SUPERNATURAL CREATURES, ARE MEANT TO AID HIM IN HIS FIGHT FOR SOCIAL CHANGE.

AMONG DR. PALMER'S SUPERNATURAL ALLIES ARE THE **GUARDIAN GODS** OF ALL SEVEN CONTINENTS.

EUROPE, THE **GUARDIAN OF THE STARS**, CAN CAUSE THE STARS TO PROVIDE GUIDANCE AND DIRECTION FOR DR. PALMER!

ONE OF DR. PALMER'S DEVICES IS A **POWER SPEEDBOAT**, WHICH CAN REACH 150 MPH AND CONVERT INTO A SMALL CAR ON LAND!

WHERE TO TURN?

WHERE SHOULD A YOUNG PERSON FACED WITH THIS ISSUE TURN? RESEARCH AND FILL OUT THE CONTACT INFORMATION BELOW.

IN YOUR CITY...

NAME: _____

PHONE: _____

EMAIL: _____

IN YOUR STATE...

NAME: _____

PHONE: _____

EMAIL: _____

IN YOUR COUNTY...

NAME: _____

PHONE: _____

EMAIL: _____

NATION-WIDE...

NAME: _____

PHONE: _____

EMAIL: _____

SUICIDE

SUICIDE IS ONE OF THE LEADING CAUSES OF DEATH AMONG CHILDREN, TEENAGERS, AND YOUNG ADULTS.[11]

PEOPLE WHO COMMIT SUICIDE ARE OFTEN SUFFERING FROM DEPRESSION, A DISORDER THAT INVOLVES EXTREME FEELINGS OF SADNESS AND HOPELESSNESS OVER A LONG PERIOD OF TIME. DEPRESSION CAN LEAD YOU TO BELIEVE THAT THINGS WILL NOT GET BETTER AND THAT LIFE IS NOT WORTH LIVING.

ESPECIALLY AMONG YOUNG PEOPLE, SUICIDE IS ALSO ASSOCIATED WITH FEELINGS OF STRESS, SELF-DOUBT, PRESSURE TO SUCCEED, FINANCIAL UNCERTAINTY, DISAPPOINTMENT, AND LOSS.[12]

TEEN PREGNANCY

DR. PALMER, DISTINGUISHED PROFESSOR AND LIFELONG SOCIAL CHANGE ACTIVIST, ENCOUNTERS A MYSTERIOUS MAN CALLED MR. JAMES. UNKNOWN TO DR. PALMER, MR. JAMES IS AN *AGENT OF AGE*. PRIOR TO HIS DISAPPEARANCE, MR. JAMES LEAVES DR. PALMER HIS WRISTWATCH.

THE WATCH, DR. PALMER DISCOVERS, CONTAINS A HIDDEN *POWER DIAL*, WHICH WILL ALLOW HIM TO TRANSFORM FROM A 75-YEAR-OLD PROFESSOR INTO A REPLICA OF HIMSELF AT AGES 20, 30, 40, AND 50. THE WATCH, ALONG WITH A RANGE OF OTHER DEVICES AND THE HELP OF SEVERAL SUPERNATURAL CREATURES, ARE MEANT TO AID HIM IN HIS FIGHT FOR SOCIAL CHANGE.

AMONG DR. PALMER'S SUPERNATURAL ALLIES ARE THE *GUARDIAN GODS* OF ALL SEVEN CONTINENTS.

ASIA, THE *GUARDIAN OF THE SUN*, CAN ASSIST DR. PALMER BY INCREASING THE SUN'S HEAT OR CAUSING TEMPORARY BLINDNESS TO OVERWHELM AN ADVERSARY!

ONE OF DR. PALMER'S DEVICES IS A *POWER JETPACK*, WHICH CAN REACH SPEEDS OF 50 MPH AND TRAVEL AT UP TO 4000 FT ABOVE LAND!

WHERE TO TURN?

WHERE SHOULD A YOUNG PERSON FACED WITH THIS ISSUE TURN? RESEARCH AND FILL OUT THE CONTACT INFORMATION BELOW.

IN YOUR CITY...

NAME: _____

PHONE: _____

EMAIL: _____

IN YOUR STATE...

NAME: _____

PHONE: _____

EMAIL: _____

IN YOUR COUNTY...

NAME: _____

PHONE: _____

EMAIL: _____

NATION-WIDE...

NAME: _____

PHONE: _____

EMAIL: _____

TEEN PREGNANCY

TEEN PREGNANCY IS VERY COMMON - IN FACT, IN THE U.S. 3 IN 10 GIRLS GET PREGNANT AT LEAST ONCE WHILE THEY ARE TEENAGERS.[15]

PREGNANCY AND BIRTH CONTRIBUTE TO HIGH SCHOOL DROPOUT RATES AMONG TEENAGE GIRLS. ONLY ABOUT 50% OF TEEN MOTHERS RECEIVE A HIGH SCHOOL DIPLOMA BY 22, WHEREAS ABOUT 90% OF WOMEN WHO DO NOT GIVE BIRTH AS TEENS GRADUATE FROM HIGH SCHOOL.[16]

TEEN PREGNANCY HAS CONSEQUENCES FOR CHILDREN BORN TO TEENS AS WELL: THEY ARE MORE LIKELY TO HAVE LOWER SCHOOL ACHIEVEMENT, TO GO TO PRISON AS TEENS, TO HAVE A CHILD AS A TEENAGER, AND TO FACE UNEMPLOYMENT AS A YOUNG ADULT.[17]

WATER SAFETY

DR. PALMER, DISTINGUISHED PROFESSOR AND LIFELONG SOCIAL CHANGE ACTIVIST, ENCOUNTERS A MYSTERIOUS MAN CALLED MR. JAMES. UNKNOWN TO DR. PALMER, MR. JAMES IS AN *AGENT OF AGE*. PRIOR TO HIS DISAPPEARANCE, MR. JAMES LEAVES DR. PALMER HIS WRISTWATCH.

THE WATCH, DR. PALMER DISCOVERS, CONTAINS A HIDDEN *POWER DIAL*, WHICH WILL ALLOW HIM TO TRANSFORM FROM A 75-YEAR-OLD PROFESSOR INTO A REPLICA OF HIMSELF AT AGES 20, 30, 40, AND 50. THE WATCH, ALONG WITH A RANGE OF OTHER DEVICES AND THE HELP OF SEVERAL SUPERNATURAL CREATURES, ARE MEANT TO AID HIM IN HIS FIGHT FOR SOCIAL CHANGE.

AMONG DR. PALMER'S SUPERNATURAL ALLIES ARE THE *GUARDIAN GODS* OF ALL SEVEN CONTINENTS.

ONE OF DR. PALMER'S DEVICES IS A *POWER JET SKI*, WHICH CAN REACH 75-100 MPH AND CONVERT INTO A MOTORCYCLE ON LAND!

NORTH AMERICA, THE *GUARDIAN OF WATER*, CAN CONTROL TIDES, BUILD GIANT WAVES, AND FLOOD RIVERS AND LAKES TO ASSIST DR. PALMER!

WHERE TO TURN?

WHERE SHOULD A YOUNG PERSON FACED WITH THIS ISSUE TURN? RESEARCH AND FILL OUT THE CONTACT INFORMATION BELOW.

IN YOUR CITY...

NAME: _____

PHONE: _____

EMAIL: _____

IN YOUR STATE...

NAME: _____

PHONE: _____

EMAIL: _____

IN YOUR COUNTY...

NAME: _____

PHONE: _____

EMAIL: _____

NATION-WIDE...

NAME: _____

PHONE: _____

EMAIL: _____

WATER SAFETY

WATER SAFETY INCLUDES THE PRECAUTIONS INTENDED TO MINIMIZE DANGER IN AND AROUND BODIES OF WATER.

WATER SAFETY IS IMPORTANT - IN FACT, DROWNING IS ONE OF THE MOST COMMON CAUSES OF ACCIDENTAL DEATH IN THE U.S.[18] DROWNING TAKES AN AVERAGE OF 3,500 TO 4,000 LIVES EVERY YEAR.[19] IN ADDITION, ABOUT 1 IN 5 PEOPLE WHO DIE FROM DROWNING ARE CHILDREN 14 AND YOUNGER.[20]

TAKING PRECAUTIONS MAKES A LARGE DIFFERENCE. FOR INSTANCE, LEARNING TO SWIM ALONE CAN REDUCE RISK OF DROWNING BY 88%.[21] EDUCATION ABOUT WATER SAFETY IS ALSO IMPORTANT IN PREVENTING DEATHS.

COVID-19

DR. PALMER, DISTINGUISHED PROFESSOR AND LIFELONG SOCIAL CHANGE ACTIVIST, ENCOUNTERS A MYSTERIOUS MAN CALLED MR. JAMES. UNKNOWN TO DR. PALMER, MR. JAMES IS AN *AGENT OF AGE*. PRIOR TO HIS DISAPPEARANCE, MR. JAMES LEAVES DR. PALMER HIS WRISTWATCH.

THE WATCH, DR. PALMER DISCOVERS, CONTAINS A HIDDEN *POWER DIAL*, WHICH WILL ALLOW HIM TO TRANSFORM FROM A 75-YEAR-OLD PROFESSOR INTO A REPLICA OF HIMSELF AT AGES 20, 30, 40, AND 50. THE WATCH, ALONG WITH A RANGE OF OTHER DEVICES AND THE HELP OF SEVERAL SUPERNATURAL CREATURES, ARE MEANT TO AID HIM IN HIS FIGHT FOR SOCIAL CHANGE.

AMONG DR. PALMER'S SUPERNATURAL ALLIES ARE THE *GUARDIAN GODS* OF ALL SEVEN CONTINENTS.

AUSTRALIA, THE *GUARDIAN OF THE MOON*, CAN HAVE THE MOON RETREAT TO CAUSE DARKNESS, CONFUSION, AND A COVER FOR DR. PALMER!

ONE OF DR. PALMER'S DEVICES IS A *POWER RADAR DEVICE*, WHICH PROVIDES HIM WITH AIR SURVEILLANCE!

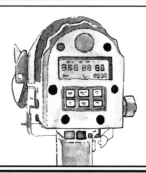

COVID-19

COVID-19 IS THE ILLNESS CAUSED BY A NEW CORONAVIRUS THAT SPREADS EASILY FROM PERSON TO PERSON.

YOU CAN BECOME INFECTED BY COMING INTO CLOSE CONTACT (WITHIN 6 FEET) OF A PERSON WHO HAS COVID-19. THE VIRUS SPREADS THROUGH RESPIRATORY DROPLETS WHEN AN INFECTED PERSON COUGHS, SNEEZES, OR TALKS. YOU MAY ALSO BECOME INFECTED BY TOUCHING A SURFACE OR OBJECT THAT HAS THE VIRUS ON IT, AND THEN TOUCHING YOUR MOUTH, NOSE, OR EYES.

IN ORDER TO PROTECT YOURSELF AND OTHERS FROM COVID-19, STAY AT HOME AS MUCH AS POSSIBLE AND AVOID CONTACT WITH OTHERS, WEAR A MASK IN PUBLIC SETTINGS, AND WASH YOUR HANDS FREQUENTLY.

WHERE TO TURN?

WHERE SHOULD A YOUNG PERSON FACED WITH THIS ISSUE TURN? RESEARCH AND FILL OUT THE CONTACT INFORMATION BELOW.

IN YOUR CITY...

NAME: _____

PHONE: _____

EMAIL: _____

IN YOUR STATE...

NAME: _____

PHONE: _____

EMAIL: _____

IN YOUR COUNTY...

NAME: _____

PHONE: _____

EMAIL: _____

NATION-WIDE...

NAME: _____

PHONE: _____

EMAIL: _____

Citations

1. Silver, David, et al. "What Factors Predict High School Graduation in the Los Angeles Unified School District." *California Dropout Research Project* accessed September 4, 2020, https://www.issuelab.org/resources/11619/11619.pdf.

2. National Center for Education Statistics. "Trends in High School Dropout and Completion Rates in the United States: 2019." Accessed September 4, 2020, https://nces.ed.gov/pubs2020/2020117.pdf.

3. Human Rights First. "Human Trafficking by the Numbers." Accessed September 4, 2020, https://www.humanrightsfirst.org/resource/human-trafficking-numbers.

4. The Human Trafficking Institute. "2018 Federal Human Trafficking Report." Accessed September 4, 2020, https://www.traffickinginstitute.org/federal-human-trafficking-report-2018/.

5. Office of the Assistant Secretary for Planning and Evaluation. "Human Trafficking Into and Within the United States: A Review of the Literature." Accessed September 4, 2020, https://aspe.hhs.gov/report/human-trafficking-and-within-united-states-review-literature#Trafficking.

6. RAINN. "Campus Sexual Violence: Statistics." Accessed September 4, 2020, https://www.rainn.org/statistics/campus-sexual-violence.

7. AAUP. "Campus Sexual Assault: Suggested Policies and Procedures." Accessed September 4, 2020, http://www.aaup.org/report/campus-sexual-assault-suggested-policies-and-procedures.

8. National Criminal Justice Reference Service. "The Campus Sexual Assault Study." Accessed September 4, 2020, https://www.ncjrs.gov/pdffiles1/nij/grants/221153.pdf.

9. Networks for Life. "Identifying and Preventing Suicide in Post-Sexual Assault Care." Accessed September 4, 2020, https://www.wcsap.org/sites/default/files/uploads/webinars/Suicide_Intervention_Recording/Networks_for_Life_for_Sexual_Assault_Care.pdf.

10. Williams, Zoe. "Sexual harassment 101: what everyone needs to know." *The Guardian*, accessed September 4, 2020, https://www.theguardian.com/world/2017/oct/16/facts-sexual-harassment-workplace-harvey-weinstein.

11. Williams, "Sexual harassment 101."

12. Riser-Kositsky, Maya. "Special Education: Definition, Statistics, and Trends." *Education Week*, accessed September 4, 2020, https://www.edweek.org/ew/issues/special-populations/index.html.

13. AACAP. "Suicide in Children and Teens." Accessed September 4, 2020, https://www.aacap.org/AACAP/Families_and_Youth/Facts_for_Families/FFF-Guide/Teen-Suicide-010.aspx.

14. AACAP, "Suicide in Children and Teens."

15. Planned Parenthood. "Pregnancy and Childbearing Among U.S. Teens." Accessed September 4, 2020, https://www.plannedparenthood.org/files/5714/0545/7055/Pregnancy_And_Childbearing_Among_US_Teens.pdf.

16. Centers for Disease Control and Prevention. "About Teen Pregnancy." Accessed September 4, 2020, https://www.cdc.gov/teenpregnancy/about/index.htm.

17. Centers for Disease Control and Prevention, "About Teen Pregnancy."

18. National Drowning Prevention Alliance. "Water Safety Facts." Accessed September 4, 2020, https://ndpa.org/5-water-safety-facts/.

19. "Water Safety Facts."

20. "Water Safety Facts."

21. "Water Safety Facts."

A Brief Biography of Professor Walter Palmer

After a tumultuous juvenile life, Professor Palmer graduated from high school and was hired by the University of Pennsylvania hospital as a surgical attendant and eventually was recruited into the University of Pennsylvania School of Inhalation and Respiratory (Oxygen) Therapy.

After his certification as an inhalation and respiratory therapist, he was hired by the Children's Hospital of Philadelphia as the Director of the Department of Inhalation and Respiratory (Oxygen) Therapy, where he spent ten years helping to develop the national field of cardio-pulmonary therapy.

In 1955, Professor Palmer created the Palmer Foundation and the Black People's University of Philadelphia Freedom School and would spend the next seventy years developing leaders for social justice nationally.

Professor Palmer has also pursued further education at Temple University for Business Administration and Communications, Cheyney State University for a Teacher's Degree in History and Secondary Education. And at age 40, acquired his juris doctorate in law from Howard University.

Between 1965 and 1995, he produced and hosted radio programs on Philadelphia WDAS, Atlantic City WUSS, and WFPG Radio, in addition to Philadelphia NBC TV 10 and New Jersey Suburban Cable Television.

In 2006, he was inducted into the Philadelphia College of Physicians as a Fellow for the body of work he had done over the past 70 years, after having spent ten (1980-1990) years as a licensed financial officer teaching poor people how to overcome poverty by saving and investing three dollars per day.

During that entire period, Professor Palmer led the Civil Rights, Black Power and Afrocentric movements in Philadelphia, around the country as well as the Caribbean and West Indies.

In the 1980s to 2015, he led the school choice movement, organized a state-wide parental school choice group which collected 500,000 petitions in 1997, which were used to create a charter and cyber school law in Pennsylvania, and in 2000 the Walter D. Palmer School was named after him.

In 1962, he created a school without walls on the University of Pennsylvania's campus and became a visiting lecturer in the Schools of Medicine, Law, Education, Wharton, History, Africana Studies, Engineering, and he currently is a lecturer in the Schools of Medicine, Social Work, and Urban Studies, where he teaches courses on American racism.

In 1969, he helped the University of Pennsylvania Graduate School of Social Work students and faculty create required courses on American racism, making the University of Pennsylvania the first school in American academia to have such courses.

In 2019, Professor Palmer was appointed to the President's Commission on commemorating the four hundred year (1619) anniversary of American slavery.

Over his many years of teaching, he has received the title of Teacher Par Excellence and has amassed over 1,000 medals, trophies, plaques, certificates, and awards for participation in multiple disciplines.

Contributors

Akinseye Brown: Lead Artist
Akinseye Brown is a native Philadelphian and full-time illustrator who has worked on multiple freelance jobs and participated in a number of gallery exhibitions in the city. He is responsible for illustrating the W. D. Palmer characters.

Eric Battle: Supporting Artist
Eric Battle is a highly sought-after Philadelphia artist with an extensive portfolio of illustration work. He is responsible for the full-page Age of Justice poster.

Aaron Beatty: Supporting Artist
Aaron Beatty is a freelance artist and illustrator from Philadelphia. He is responsible for the Guardian illustrations for Africa, Asia, North and South America, the Artic, and Australia.

Walter D. Palmer: Story
Walter D. Palmer is responsible for creating the story and structure of the Age of Justice project.

Francesca Ciampa: Art Design and Layout
Francesca Ciampa is an undergraduate student at the University of Pennsylvania. She is responsible for layout and for illustrating the power devices and the Guardian character for Europe.

W. D. Palmer Foundation Hashtags

1. #racedialogueusa
2. #racismdialogueusa
3. #atriskchildrenusa
4. #youthorganizingusa
5. #stopblackonblackusa
6. #newleadershipusa
7. #1619commemorationusa
8. #africanslaveryusa
9. #indigenouspeopleusa
10. #afrocentricusa
11. #civillibertiesusa
12. #civilrightsusa
13. #humanrightsusa
14. #saveourchildrenusa
15. #parentalschoolchoiceusa
16. #wearyourmaskusa
17. #defeatcovid19usa
18. #socialdistanceusa

19

Printed in the United States
By Bookmasters